Of Everything
I Once Loved

Robert Paul Taylor

Of Everything
I Once Loved

First Edition

WWW.STREETFAMEBOOKS.COM

Chuck Kissy Forever

Cover Photo by Garret Suhrie 2015

Born, Bled & Printed in the U.S.A

Also available by

Robert Paul Taylor

DRIFTING

PARIS IN FLAMES

LIKE THIS

ALL OUT WAR

SOLITARY MAN

IMPASS

BURN ASH RISE

ITHICA

SKYLINE

THE GARDEN

"As artists, we are married to our work.
We have a commitment to it
for better or worse, in sickness and in health,
until death do us part."

-Julia Cameran

TABLE OF HEART BREAK & HAPPINESS

Running (Brand New Day)..1
From The Beginning...4
Of Everything I Once Loved..5
Under The Trees We Lay..7
Sailing Away...9
Repairing The Repairs...11
There Is A Place In My Heart..12
All Eyes On Me..14
Bodies Just Pile...15
This Rotting House...17
Return To Sender..18
Staring At The Fork...20
Steering Away From The Rivers Side..22
Daddy Come Closer...24
The Canyon She Sits Upon...26
We Dance..28
Nails Smear...29
Bird Fly Free..30
Shaken Head U-Turn..34
Gut Instinct, Left..36
Battle Star Gallactica...38
Allow Me To Introduce Myself...41
Displaced...43
Already She Speaks...54
Rearranging Popsicle Sticks Alone...56
Two Years Away..57
Funerals And Flat Tires..59
Grave Digger Slave..61
The Girl Who Wants to Know..64
Closed Eye Swan Dive..66
Look To The Sky...68
Sitting At El Matador..69
The Changing Seasons Of My Life...71
Someone We'll Never Meet..74
Been The Killer..75

She Was Dying Her Hair……………………………………….....76
Sitting Duck……………………………………………………….78
Blackened…………………………………………………………..80
No One See's Me This Way……………………………………….81
Haven't I Been Good To You……………………………….......84
Hurting The Ones You Love……………………………………..85
In The Orchard Mumbling………………………………………86
806 And The Floor Dying……………………………………......89
806 (Continued)………………………………………………….92
Like My Father……………………………………………………94
Ms. James………………………………………………………….95
A Moment In Time………………………………………….......97
How Sorry I Am…………………………………………………..98
X……………………………………………………………………99
Bursting In Air…………………………………………….........100
Koi Fish Swimming……………………………………………..102
Outside Your House……………………………………….......104
On The Edge Of A Continent………………………………….105
Flight Forty Five…………………………………………………107
The Corners of My Eyes………………………………………..108
The Oncoming Exit……………………………………………..110
Loading Clips……………………………………………………112
Kialani…………………………………………………………….113
Brothers In Arms………………………………………………..115
But Like My Mother…………………………………………….118
This Side of the Lake……………………………………………121
The Scent of Rich Soil………………………………………….123
In Liquid Form Creating……………………………………….125
A Box by the Door………………………………………………128
The Way the Shovel Falls……………………………………….130
Reseal Everything……………………………………………….132
The Child Inside………………………………………………...135
Destroy You………………………………………………………137
Sun Yellow……………………………………………………….139
Fall Children…………………………………………………….145
One Day In October……………………………………………..147
When The Night Comes…………………………………………148

Man of Valor...150
Behind My Eyes..152
Silences Of Beauty..154
Newcomers & Prostitues...159
The Way You Say My Name...166
Chicken Legs of Taboo...168
Just Look Black...170
Seat Belts In The Night...173
From Your Mouth..176
Oh Birdy...177
Inside Your Arms...178

Forward

Avocado green jagged palm trees mumble amongst each other quietly in the early afternoon sway of summer. Their strong-caked earth elephant trunks stand still in preserverance. The solstice just yesterday and I feel the revolution of another dance around the sun settling in on my mindset.

Los Angeles is often like a time warp with every day clear blue skies, comforter temperatures, its amazing one can separate the seven blocks of a calendar.

I have my computer set up at my desk just facing north into the Hollywood Hills so I get equally aqua sky, varietals of palm tree's and the Russian neighbor girl who does yoga poses in her panties on the rooftop across the way in late afternoon in my sight.

I lived here before she did, so I certainly did not set it up that way. I mean, why do I have to move my work desk just because beauty has shown her self in mismatched underwear?

I can't tell if I should feel lucky to have such a young pretty girl in downward dog position just in eye's view or I should feel slightly violated that in my more mature, concerned years of adult hood, this girl can peer right into my very bedroom with me googgling at her between the sheer white cotton curtains.

Yes, I look. But if you don't want me to look, don't sun salutation in a thong facing my wandering mind's eye. Actually, go ahead honey, get your yoga in, after all, birds were meant to be enjoyed in their natural habitat.

Earlier last night, I arrived at the sweat lodge in Oxnard, and I ran into my old life partner around the fireplace. I have been praying this way on the red road for 9 years now. I first brought her to this house that was built for the stone people and she has accustomed the ceromony way of life into her own.

At one point in time, it was our life. Praying, kneeling and consoling. I remember one day after ceromony we were laying out in the grass after an Native American give away ceromony outside under the tree's and our sweat leader Wolf walked by and looked down at us intertwined and grinned, "ahh, now that is good medicine."

Good medicine is what great love is. That was great medicine. Was a grand summer that year. That brings peace to mind, to have shared something so sacred, so positive with someone whom I love dearly.

She gave me a big hug and just smiled at me long and pensive.

I thought she was going to offer me something sweet and consoling when she just grinned and said, "you have grey hair uni-brows," in a playful child like voice.

Thank you my dear. Yes, time is having its way with me as it does with everything else.

I wanted to add that I had no one to pluck them as of recently, but thought that would be too self indulgent, so I just took a mental note to take care of it when I arrived back home. I smiled back at the girl I once loved, and way time had kissed her frame as well. Her face seemed longer with added pearl, her hair felt slightly less buoyant than the days we used to laugh in.

Still, she had many years to go before even the slightest landing of a crow could even touch her youth. Which made me think about our time spent together in love. What a beautiful woman whom I got to share some of the best of my life with.

We prayed, we laughed, we fucked, we plotted, pummeled and traveled. In the end, we bent and cried. I found her in a cabaret restaurant one night just a few days after the season finale of Lost, at the end of May, somewhere, towards the end of this book, which was years even from now.

In the beginning years of my recovery, words, thoughts and poems seem to flow from every inch of my hands at every waking hour. Time has taken the best of us and now years have come and gone since I have sat down and gotten these out to fly. Letting them age like wine always seems to do the trick. Pour a little life over them to collect some dust.

Kind of like when you have a certain shirt you bought in your closet, you haven't worn it before and you wonder why you even acquired it in the first place. Then months later, somehow after arguments, trials and seasons, one day you put the shirt on and finally it is done. It's your new favorite shirt and you wear it for weeks.

With all that being said, I'm not quite sure I need to do any grand set ups for my life's work.

I don't quite remember what grand gesture I wanted to make at that time in my life.

Jail was a few months behind me; the fear of monthly probation visits and keeping a very straight and narrow edge on all that I do was definitley a habitual condition. When I wanted to leave town, I needed a written note to my probation officer, with dates, employer names, locations, travel companions and work reasons.

Drive to the east side of Los Angeles, turn the paper in and wait for it to be signed off. Those days were successful. The travel came and gone. The relationships as well. Time seems to get the best of me just as I am sure it gets the best of you.

Oh boy, here comes the downward dog.

I'm sure she likes the attention, or just in the back of her mind wondering if anyone is watching. It's like the woman who strokes a few extra lashes, tightens up her blouse one button loose and wears a bra one cup size too small, then whispers under her breathe 'perv" to the man she passes on the street stretching his eyes for one lovely glance of a bouncing bosom.

We play the game for each other.
We know exactly what we are doing.

Anyway, honesty has always been the reason people seem to read and honesty is where I need to stay centered. So for honesty's sake, it has been quite a few years since I have really remembered the big picture. That big circle up in the stars, with all the spirit guides, planning this earthly visit. We named each other, took our roles and leaped into the abyss. Somewhere between the oceans and airplanes, lips, hips and baggies, I can't seem to find my script.

So without bullshitting my way through an unneccessary foreword, I give you what I give to the world the best.

Brass honesty.

I have always been attracted to the darkness. Pulled magnetically. It once consumed my every pore. The longer I stay drug free & clean, the less appealing it seems to be on every level. I think these are some of the last days of darkness and the first days of holy shit there is a world after capitalistic consummation.

The prepubescent days of rebirth after the American dream has lost it's luster. The days when we see there is light ahead, there is hope ahead, there is love ahead, there is yet another beautiful sunrise and moonlight sky to approach.

There will always be my fleeting moments of comfort in the past. Lustful sword fighting will always be apart of who I am. But, there is more. I am still finding the the roads and treasures daily.

Life is a grand journey and I hope to be on it long and hard for years to come. I wish you same. With the sun at your face and the wind on your heels, may the lessons be often and discoveries abundant. Try to stay honest. Atleast with yourself and those that truly matter.

After all, what else do we really have in life but our experiences, opinions and service to others?

I'm desperately trying not to say it, but in that desperation I suffocate that which I truly need to release. Dear Russian yoga girl stretching your quads upside-down on the rooftop with your towel and water.

Yes, I know you see me watching you. Yes, I want to fuck you.

At least I think that I do. Buying you matching underwear would be a pretty high priority if that were to happen. Would that be of service to her? See, there's the pause they talk about. The fucking pause. I remember when I didn't have the pause. Life was much more spontaneous. Seemed richer, in hindsight. But it wasn't.

It's my inability to take personal responsibility that which I discovered along the way, that I was merely the one, responsible for causing most of my life's problems.

Maybe I should put my focus on something more constructive.

Others, right. Helping others.

Helping others is the best way I know to get out of my own head. To get out of my own way. The mental surrender. Release.

I have the title of this book tattooed on each of my forearms. One side reads Of Everyhing I Once Loved and the other Letting Go.

I used to work in a restaurant with my sleeves rolled up just perfectly as borders above my tattoos. There are two kinds of people in the world. One type would look at the script and say, "oh god, that's so sad, what about your mom? You don't love your mom? and I would just smile.

The other would read it and look up after a moment of reflection and smile peacefully, "That's right. Beautiful." Those people understood surrender. Those people also understood the bouillabaisse.

We are not in control. Life is driving us. The world is spinning and we can do nothing about it. The goal is to let go. To let it breathe. Because life always wins.

The goal:

To avoid the fears from the voices & vices, the future tripping and the consummation of an American lifestyle riddle with confusion.

To love freely like I have never sensed dissipation, and to travel this fucking rock. Pack a bag and find some playful afternoon romance on a long train ride. Get on a plane and get the hell out of this place once in a while.

See the world, taste its food, its culture. Learn phrases in another language. Forget timezones, confuse phone cards, search for wifi just to call upon your loved ones.

Find your way in a distant land, after being lost for hours on end, and once again, you will find yourself.

It's so easy to get locked into a way of life. Sometimes so hard to break free from it. The fear they pump into us about getting up and going. But it's a facade. The world is a beautiful place.

There is just so much out there besides our daily routine.

Feel the world.

There are so many corners to turn and jump from.

So with that being said, I need not say more.

-Robert Paul Taylor
June 22, 2015

Of Everything I Once Loved

Letting Go

-Running

When I was a kid
I used to run home from school
Eager to get away from class
All the kids
Used to hate the way those little chairs felt
Creak of the classroom
Grand clock-tock
Tick-tock

Run away from home
When you can't take anymore
Parents fighting
Plates breaking
Little headphones loud
Little TV louder
Wasn't big enough to drown much out
Run away from friends
Run from jobs
Run away from cities
Run away from this country
See the world
From a distance
Far
Far away

Breathtaking
Another place
Another language
Distant time zone
The faces look so different
Food
Smells
Cities
People walk the streets

So many people fill our heads
So many voices
So loud
Shades of colors
Images broken pieces of life
Memories
Too much to take in one breathe

So slowly
Breathe
Again
Then again

Guess I've run away from everyone
A target
A place to run and hide

These days I just run to run
A place to hide in our head
The way the world fills our eyes
Life pounds in our ears
Watching the world bounce up and down
The sun in our breathe
Oceans in our spit
Watching the world spin on

Finding our way again
In a new city
The world looks so different
Without you here
The pain of memories
Just get on the train
Fall asleep
Wake up in a new place
A new city
New time zone

Sometimes
It's anywhere but here
Sometimes
We fall asleep
We want another chance
Another shot at getting what we need
Another chance
At loving you better
At loving us better
Hoping
To wake up
To a brand new day
12/17/08

-From The Beginning-

Feels to good to be true
A new life with you
New friend
Found you again
Alone
I am
Happy a clam
Don't need anyone
Just a space
With god
Your face
Alive
I cry
Tears of joy
Oh boy
This is bliss
The juice of life
So rich
So pure
So simple
12/19/08

-Of Everything I Once Loved-

Letting go of it all
Watching it all fall
Ready to fly
Scouring grounds
Pecking
Searching
Acting out
Children grow up
Deviated plans
Harder to stand

So long
All this
Letting go
Of everything
I once trusted
Just to be a man

Talk all day
Feed - hay
Munching away
Turn - betray
Her

Shouldn't the martyr
For life expelled
Tell the difference
Between nature or nurture
Fantasy
Or way of life
The strife
To kill
Finally succumb to man
Taken in hands

Leaving women behind
Solace - run
I belong
Fighting the fear for so long
Help
As I cap this bottle
Sealed letters - away
Throwing it all - today
Into the ocean
Letting go
Of everything I once loved
12/28/08

-Under The Trees We Lay-

So here we lay again
Subtle
Watching you crawl
Comfort
Of the night

Cold hair winter
Brushed clean again
Long legs December
Now gone
A new year
Upon us again

Into your arms
Stretching
Towards tomorrow
In time lips
May touch light
So many ways changed

My lover blurs
No escape
Just retreat
Stepping back a foot to see
This is who I am

Finding the comfort
Under this comforter
Hands caress back
Spreading open
A new year awaits

So many things to feel
So many places to find
This space sacred

Here in the dark
This is just who we are

Tonight you drink from me
Feeding you
I see
Stroking fears
Keeping warm ears
Thighs soft
Falling knees
I surrender

Sky open January
Watch you tower
Making rain
Feeding seeds
All upon me falls
Blood of life
Envelops my world
Licking - splashing down
Tunnel we tumble
No more I fumble
Around the walls of the mind
Just breathing next to you
Curled up in a ball

Falling together peacefully
For this is
Who we really are

For a new year has arrived
So plain - so simple
Darkness is warm
01/02/09

-Sailing Away-

Deep magenta smears
Sand upon the horizon
The ocean
She breathes

Gentle waves crash the shore
Water splashing dance floor
Undertow reveals - shimmer
White clouds salt bubble smooth
The ocean
She reaches for me

Each wave a bit further back
She is losing this tide
As for tonight
The moon pulls us away

Take a step closer
Let her win
She gently touches our feet
Playing this game with mother earth
How I long for your touch

Watching the red ball
Sink the skyline
Earth cools
Colors of blue
Grey sand
Soft hands
Today
It is just me who is going down

The sun
She is merely passing us around

Traffic blurring
Cars churn - crawl
Winding down - sunset
Yellow lines
Red lights - clear
Eyes smear
Pulling my scarf closer
I know it will be dark again soon
And my mind will be too

Watching the ocean reach out for me
I wince at her losing stretch
I remind her that tomorrow
She will win again
When the moon lets us go
We can out stretch our arms
And touch dry land

Until then
Into the night we sail
Slowly losing this fight
Heading towards the moon
01/07/09

-Repairing The Repairs-

You came to visit
So I cleaned my house
We talked after all these years
At the edge of the ocean
The water we walked in
Separated my life
In your eyes
Letting you give me advice
Throws me for a loop
Seeing the holes in my recovery
Seeing the dust on my bookshelf
Asking me the most basic of questions
Leaves me baffled why I haven't answered
To myself
Knowing this round again
Needing to dismantle the little
I have sewn
Start this sweater again
For the arms are too short
The aim not far enough
Selling myself cheap again

Driving away I speed faster faster
Breaking the glass on my shelf
Dissolving tablets
Loosening belt
Making changes again
Changing the way I see the world

01/18/09

-There Is A Place In My Heart-

Scared to go further
Ashamed of the past
Afraid to ask
For your help

Hopefully - one day will be better
Hopefully - one day trust more
Hopefully - one day trust myself
Hopefully - tomorrow

Embarrassed to know
Letting you in
So close
Insides
Race back forth
See behind curtains
Machines drag long
Clinking - clacking

Need oil
Letting you closer
I just might
Not be able
Barely know myself
Let alone
Give this to you
Too soon
Maybe we should
Part now
Someone better than me

Younger - brighter
Pocket change
With out - scars - shame
Go now

Before I cry too
Walk away

Finger fuck your phone
Play online - set the tone
Speed down the five
Techno jive
Clicking tongue
Smoke & stick
Just miss me
When the summer
She comes
And just know
That I think of you too
Thinking of you too
Little duck
01/22/09

-Bodies Just Pile-

Coming too close
Step back
Step forward
Retreat
Your pain
Distance
Created
Fear of tomorrow
Shames today
Singing scars
The gentle ways
We were told
Not to be afraid
Days of my youth
In my head
Your face shines & smile
Fear bigger
Than the sun
Clouded mind
Gather round
The black box
Locked away
Happiness
Another day
Key unturned
Body in the grave
Shovel - hand
Another lover - slain
Bodies just pile
Night falls again
Slowly retreating
Through darkness
All around
Inside my head
01/23/09

14

-This Rotting House-

Hidden slivers & lye
Embedded
I built
Truth soured
The sun
The lie
In darkness
The foundation we build

Soiled rotten beliefs
Sinking
Finally breaking
House shifting
Windows bay
Ceilings creak
Doors never quite shut
Root of evil
Guidance of the sun
Grows into man
Forever

Living upon slivers
Forever
Embedded
Crushing
My lovers invisible pain
Wondering
Where these cuts come from
Wondering
How this can be
The eyes
Oh the tricks they play
Never letting us truly see
Behind the walls
Under the carpeted floors

Downstairs
In the garage
Underneath
The foundation
These slivers
Lay embedded
Embedded in everything
I have ever touched
01/23/09

-Return To Sender-

Sent a letter to you
Approval
Reason to share - intimate
Trained - open up
Doesn't really matter how
Or why
I can show someone
Something

One person
Whom to tell it all
Show the inside

Picture on the wall
Behind the pictures on the walls
So I send a letter to you
To read between the lines
Show me some signs
I just can't see

Because - standing too close
Too close - to see the glaze
Too close - to see the shimmer
Of the sky fallen - dark
Send this letter to you
Waiting - patiently by a door
Waiting - to send this letter to you
01/23/09

-Staring At The Fork-

Mind like pendulum
Back & forth swing
Indecisiveness kills
One step forward
Two steps back
Relationships crack
Missing
Killing fields
Blood seeps
Watch black crows
Scream across the sky
Child like fuss
Gulping
Swallows & ponder
Thoughtfully
Keep
Indecisive

Alluded point
Weekends fall
All over
Just to walk home
Sinister ways
Of yesterday
To realize
The mind often broken

Cuckoo clocks
Screaming
Lungs collapsing
Cold skin
Painting the walls
Making mistakes
Beverages spill
Pulling nails

Pulling teeth
In the distance
We all stare
Watching the world go by
Eyes wide shut
Slowly keeping myself
Indecisive
1/25/09

-Sitting Much To Close-

Sitting peaceful
Goosebumps
Tiny prickles
Farm of cacti up your legs
Lashes bat
Pain behind those contacts
Perfect makeup
Perfect hair
Perfect breakup
Let me glare
A second guess
Bumper car arms
Tension of thick
Corners
Eyes
Stare
Already ripping your clothes
Inside we swing
Tugging lips
Smearing makeup

Trying a future
With these
Drying sutures
Between us
For you are
Fine china
Don't expect
You'll have much sympathy
For my grieving
The price to pay
Fo an early departure
Ending too soon
Out of fear
Afraid - future - come

Way up ahead
This must be right
Even as I want to fuck you all night
More than lust
Thrust
Of tongues
Chasing lungs
Remember the Indian
Told me
The mind - dangerous
Only - heart - trust
Listen to the part
Beat so rhythmic
Beats so fast
Beat - drum
Heart just hums
Away
In peace
Pumping blood
As we sit together
In silence
As we sit together
And pray
01/28/09

-Steering Away From The Rivers Side-

And so we meet again
After all these years gone by
The room painted different
The eyes the same
The way the light hits your face
Seeing angles I've never noticed before
Looks like I'm not the only one
Tasting the kiss of time
Watching your mind
Still trying
To control everything within reach
Your tentacles wrap around me
Again
The punishment of seclusion
With you
Secluded in this conversation
Trapped in this bubble
The pirate ship you steer
Splashes the waters over my bow
Seeing you for you
For the first time
In so long
Looks like I've had enough again
Just a few hours in
I already feel sea-sick
The boat already too much to take
Thinking about my exit
So soon this visit should end
Knowing that you haven't changed
As much as I would have liked you too
No I don't want to be on your boat
I don't want to sail on your waters
The coast of my shores are suited
Better for me these days
The years gone past

Have brought to me too much bliss
To even start to miss
The way we used to be
The old friend you see in me
Is still in there
And I know he is still inside of you
But the demon in the room
Is just too big for me to move past
The growling of control
And manipulation
Makes me want to push away
Take my little oars
And push off
Back to my side of the island
I head
With a headache full of ache
The voices take so long to escape
The resonance of your voice in my dreams
Awakens me to silent screams
Escaping your tentacles harder these days
Than the ones that have past
Guess I have just enough gas
To get home safely tonight
Happy to know
I won't be returning to you
Anytime so soon
So long old friend
Won't see you again too soon
02/07/09

-Daddy Come Closer-

Thinking of my dear old friend
The man of every hour
The power of hard work
The will that won't let me give in
The power within
You instilled like iron
Wrought beams hanging overhead
Missing the grey hairs on your head
The way you used to chuckle
So much advice I could sure use

That push to shove me the hard way
Deep blue eyes seeing the world
Your own way
Look how much has changed
These days father
The world has twisted for the better
Yet just a day again passing
Feeling your warmth around my sides
Miss you so much daddy
The world has changed again

I am spinning with it too
So fast we walk through
This dream unfolding
Before my very eyes
Wish you could see me
Growing in strides
Remembering our final conversations
About wishing you could see
Who I marry and have children with
I can't wait to see either dad
I can't wait to see either
The way tomorrow blows me in
Resting to sleep within

This peace of mind I have to bring myself
Hoping your happy in your new world
The chores of the golden sword
A builder forever
A lover in time
Missing the way you made me smile
The encouragement from
A man to a man
Who can understand
The world in which you raised me
The boy has become a man
Now the man grows old
Walking in the boots you left behind
Paying the debts to society
You make me wind up
And unravel out
Towards the future so bright
Missing you so much tonight
My father of my dreams
Come to me tonight
With high beams and hugs

Send me a signal from above
Can you hear my thoughts at night
Can you see this little light
Knowing one day again
Your hand I shall hold
Watching this movie
Called life unfold
02/07/09

-The Canyon She Stands Upon-

To rejoice the night
Rain plummet down
Upon my face
Around my feet
Splashing
Oh raining hour
Wash me away
Winter crawled again
Year of change
Turns recounting
Memories
Laughing - love
I think I'll let her stay

World so small
Heart so big
Peace you bring
Within
Oh baby just let go
Sleep next to me this way

Laughing tell me
My side of the bed
Is on top of you
Sure know me well
Dig into you dwell
Surrounded jovial
Patient
All these years
Come upon us again
Rain brings a clean shower
Another romantic hour
A feast of you
Devouring love
Kiss the dove on my arm

Lick my warm scars
Breathing neck
Kissed like children
Playing past ten
Sleeping den
Beneath the hills
Of Hollywood
Upon you again

I am waiting
Father in my sleep
Lover at my feet
Craft in print
Sins in air
Give it all
Just to have this to hold onto

Just to have you with me
Just to let you know
Our love still grows
The garden just glows
With memories
Of the best
Inhale - ingest
Take your hands to mine
Pray kind
Worship us
Forever and ever
We shall be this way
02/07/09

-We Dance-

Here in this room
Feel so real
Place where I laid
Day you left
World turned
Inside out
Flipped out
Srongest layer of armor
No one can ever take away

Gave me this final gift
Laying here again
Moons have passed
Sun so round
Grass grows greener
Right side of the hill
So much from the mind
Fountains of youth
We dance

Forever holding place
For your love
Forever expand
Consciousness
Without identity
Without
The nets of youth
Take leaps
Take bounds
Today we rise again
02/10/09

-Nails Smear-

And so I hit the stage
A feather in the wind
This way I just blow
Facing the lens again
Facing the world so bright
Just this skin holds might
The times to fight have past
Now the future lies so pleasant
All these grains of sand
Fallen so gracefully
Like the leaves from the trees
Together we leave this garden

Hearing your voice again through the line
Spin me round record player lover
One more time
Caressing your words
Too much I still inflate
Remembering the artist inside
The way I was as a child
The place where animals run wild
Be with me tonight my love
Back up on stage again
Finally complete
So paint these nails
Smear this liner
Watch the world flash like lenses
Take this pen
Hurry this mess again
02/21/09

-Bird Fly Free-

And I once had to
Give it all away just to be alone
And I once had to
Let you go to let myself grow this way
And I once had to
See myself without you in everyway

Just to have someone to come home to
Just to have something to hold onto
To be the person I knew I could be
Now you speak to me again
So many things you could say
So many ways to show your growth
But still you just focus on the negative
Taking credit for all that is beautiful
So toxic in everyway
So unpleasant stay

It must feel amazing to know
That the whole world
Wants to be just like you
Everything everyone ever created
Must have been your idea
So amazing how you see yourself
In everything that I do
Taking all the credit for me you do

It must be so easy
To live in your head of greed
To be the person everyone wants you to be
Too childish to let a bird fly free
To afraid to let the sky just be
Take from me nothing
And I ask of you the same

Just leave me to be again
For I can't let you in this close
You're just too toxic for my being
Too controlling
Too demeaning

And I once had to
Give it all away just to be alone
And I once had to
Let you go to let myself grow
And I once had to
See myself without you in everyway
02/21/09

Brick by brick I built this life

Painting the sky blue so true

-Shaken Head U-Turn-

Cleared slate
Shower scrubbed
Combed hair
The journey to you

Requested drugs
The two truths
Sex
& booze
Too much for me to use

Refuse the offer
Can't deny
Can't you see
Don't get high
That way
Whether choice or yours
Won't be that dumb

Body of the night
Champagne bright
Bubbles
Nipples
Fresh peel
Far off land

A slap from my hand
Can't do it that way
Just won't
No sucker for lust

Today, do too much
Just go back home
Sleep the sleep
Of the righteous

I am stronger
Strong enough
The right decision
The right incision
In this paper thin relationship

Probably won't even feel
This tiny little paper cut
I can't even find on my hand
02/23/09

-Gut Instinct, Left-

Getting lost again
Giving away
Just anyone
Respect deserve
Integrity of self worth
Always take
Cheapest route
Most expensive moments

Child inside
Cry
Reaching for everything
Validation
Proof
Worthy

Close the roads
Seclude
Savor
Free bird cage
Truly amaze
Days of the summer
Sunrise alone

Winter months cover
Protect unwanted world
Child be born
No one else in the world
Can save me

Shovel again in hand
Digging sand
Shoveling
Once again
Digging

Escape the mind
The power of god
Meditating
Above

Only god
Can show
Not the billboard
My dick
Or the voice on the phone
I found it once

Now I search again alone
Finding another way home
02/23/09

-Battlestar Gallactica-

Battle star Gallactica
Take me away
Today
Down depths
Oceans mind
We go
Traveling away
I know
Just a fragment
Of my imagination

Strong as elephant tusk
Lack money
Bust
Halves
Bitter sharp
Brittle bitten
Half lick
Chap lip
Biting winter cold
All alone
Together in this ship
We sink

Battle star Gallactica
Rope astray
Take me away
Safety of dock
Anchor my comfort
Deep restful sleep
Feathers seep
All over the floor
Air pockets no more
Just cold stiff sheets
Jarred awaken

Stiffened - startled - charred
Cold - scarred
Feeling - scarcity
Battle star begun

Lost in mind
Lust another hour
Ahead into time
Squinted eyesd
Stirred lime
Prepping
For the garden
I always end up
In the end

Battle star Gallactica
Take me away
Go deep today
Relatives - friends
Spread fear in the world
Mirrors broken
Clock still
Blood hands
Naked stands
Game finished
Watching the grass grow in the rain
Swimming pain
Oceans
Reasons of lie
Weight of the city
Fear of the world

Failed - soiled
Turning mud
Water rising above
Shins
On the bow

Of my Battle star Gallactica
Water rising
Limbs
Face grins
Gnarls Could have succeeded
Everything I ever had
Artist life
Live in love
Harmony

Peace & bliss
Today just miss
Regularity - routine
Motion of others
Sound of desks
Squeeking tin
Lunchtime din
Laughter

A pin drop could shatter
Eye dry September
Mental pain
Sun settling sunset
As my ship slowly sinks
Battle star Gallactica
Oh take me away
03/10/09

-Allow Me To Introduce Myself-

If the sky bleeding grey
Has come to be clear
The writers block chipped away
The black steer of the day
Rich and deep
The velvet of my mind
Lay before us all again
I am free to let this muse run

Free again and found a way
At home alone I feel so strong
Feeling the intimacy of this pain
The life long body bag search for love
The private investigator he never sleeps
Inside the office all night he stays

Always searching for new ways
Finding true love a mission in life
Forget a wife
Let's just find a new lover
For old time's sake
Shake the bottle
Spill a few pills
Let's burn a drag
Share a few grams then grab
Some rest for the night
The black beauty of life
She has just begun

Feels good to be home
Back in the saddle alone
Knowing just maybe
Just maybe
This may be a coupe ride home
To the end

The backseat for pictures and books
Lingers and looks
I steer with my knees
As I sharpen these hooks
For the big fish are harder to catch
And this new bait won't last
Prepare world you'll soon see
Oh dear world
You're in for a real treat with me
03/10/09

-Displaced-

You found me today
Digging here in the dirt
Naked newborn
World shines bright
Sky
Flashing past lies
Melted ground
Ironman working
Pounding fists
The world
Striking
Delicately
Reasons corrosive
Displaced here on planet earth
My womb
Seasons
As they change
So do thy eyes
Reflecting color of the sky
You found me here
A new born growing kid
Searching for the reasons
Why
Man does the things he does
Displaced here on planet earth
Searching for the reasons
Why
I hurt myself this way
Needing
Exploring
Depths of mind
Stillness of the world
Forever kept untouched
Land too futile to spoil
The rotten soil of despair

Somehow I breathe this air
Like the mammals found near
The human species so clear
So defiant a race
So willing to lose this place
Killing the fields
Killing the trees
Killing all that is beautiful
The peace from our ancestors
Slowly grinding
Makes no sense
Clenching teeth
Writhing feet
In this fetal position
In the black of the night
Just near the oceans end
The place where you have found me
Displaced here on planet earth
03/13/09

And to what was everything

Without you here by my side

Waiting on forever to reach this light

Focused a lifetime with this insight

The beauty of letting go

Of everything we once touched

Of everything once strived to be

The beauty of letting go

Of everything I once longed to be

-Already She Speaks-

Crisp air
Short mercury
Tiny lanterns
Rose petal gutters
A month of activity
Death to birth
Physically mental
My sister
She bears again life

The month my dear friend left
Just a week before my fathers death
The woman
Bears the child of life
Creating happiness
Inside the world
Feeding marrow & bone
Blood filled home

Body full of love
Inside our temple of doves
Watching her grow wise
Color of the skies
Husband stands near
Feet so dear
Belly weight
Empty water
Newborn blood spilled

Hospital rooms fill
Perfect breathe
Glimpsing
Smiling amazement
Creative wife
Creating life

World offers
Of this baby girl
Newest niece
Wrapped in fleece
Glowing unity
Welcome to the family
Little one
03/16/09

-Rearranging Popsicle Sticks Alone-

Popsicle sticks scatter the board
One by one the spaces grow
Perfecting the maze of life
Spaces in which to crawl
White lines smear the light
Imperfections so beautiful
Fingernails blackened by love
Hearts bleeding from above
The world drips into me
This way

Kitchen sink barren
Music fluttering the room
The sound of growth
Slowly crackle
Happiness once again
Seemingly appears
Childlike we play

But we won't be saved
The night young as this love
So much darkness still to come
Guess I'll just keep going
Until this paint runs dry
Squeezing the tube of life
Making another smear
Blotting canvas
Creating life
03/19/09

56

-Two Years Away-

The years I have toiled past
Clear and present entrances to the grandest
Entrance of my life
The purest form of love
Finally peeling its way through
Moss on the walls
Steam of the glass
The life time I have survived
Circa of now
The only true moment that ever matters
Eternal moment called now

Finally I have seen the goals of my thoughts
The two years since 'paris'
The two years since 'toil'
The two years past
Since the last time I passed
A bag of narcotics to that woman
The beautiful and deadly blonde
My last drug deal haunts me
No more
No need to settle this score
Finally I have some distance
From the last town
No reason today to frown
All needs met
All bills paid
Emotions stayed
On the path most righteous

The war is over
& I can live like a general
With wars stories
& books
Always a friend to crooks

But no longer a victim
To my mind
Alone I stand
& together we fall
Unity makes us tall
Pride and faith
In God's will we trust
Today one step at a time
One day in time
Created this sweet wine
Of life and love
Of faith and honor
Today we rest among the victorious
Today is a beautiful day
03/23/09

-Funerals and Flat Tires-

The old saying goes
A friend in need is a friend in deed
All though these past deeds have already
Been paid
You still act like I owe you a slave
Like you did so much for this life
I have created

You take credit for every little thing
That happens on the planet
Devoid of free will
We all just want to be like you
In control and chubby
My old friend's hubby
Never a hostage again will I be
Too you I see
Wincing at your insecure ways
The text message you saved
Sending me hatred through the wires
Do you really perspire at the thought
Of my success
Do you really wish everything you say
Was true
Knowing that if you really deeply
Didn't care
You wouldn't stop to stare
You wouldn't say a word
Because the things we don't care about
Don't even cross our minds
Or our phones
or our mail
So slow like a snail
I still crawl forward
Advancing on all levels you see
Full of steam like a tug boat

Ready to carry these dreams across
The sea
Across the street
Cross these seams and
Forever let this past go
God it's so funny
How dramatic you can be
Attaching everything that ever happened
To anyone to me
Maybe this friendship is long and dead
Maybe we should just save these phone calls
For funerals and flat tires
So go now perspire
In your broken hearted sorrow
Oh how I let you down today
I can't imagine any other way
03/30/09

-Grave Digger Slave-

Seems as if the distance was greater
The quiet time we spent apart
Felt less painful
Than the realism of phone calls
Allowed
Yet calling on no one
We seem to do
Left you another message
Just the other day
Knowing you wouldn't return
Your love nor the message

Seems as if the distance was greater
The quiet time we spent apart
Knowing in my heart
Here I stand
Five years later
Burying you again
This garden full of so many trenches
Dug
Yet still this body just changes holes
Moving you around in the night
Like a grave digger
Slave bigger than last
My heart breaks too fast
Maybe not breaking these days
Just tiny cracks and shingles
This friendship salty like Pringles
& bitter

Seems as if the distance was greater
The quiet time we spent apart
The sweet names you once called
Me now gone
There were too intimate

Too fond, now just my name
Barely you speak
Barely into the phone
Leaving me alone
Again
Where I belong
Away from the world
Away from this place
That I have been so many times before

Seems as if the distance was greater
The quiet time we spent apart
Of every page I ever wrote was for you
Knowing this time it could be true
Realizing I have done this to myself
Over and over and over again
This time I must let us end
For I know tonight
You really are just not coming home
03/30/09

& everything will have its end

-The Girl Who Wants To Know-

So we lay here naked in bed
Talking about life instead
Its these lips we touch
No lighters to fuss
Just the continents flicker
In our minds eyes

Of years to come
Of those past
Thinking of ways to better the world
Maybe a doctor
Or philanthropy
This long awaited atrophy

It was upon me
So shall it be to you
Caressing your flesh I do
Porcelain skin so taunt
Looks of exploration
We flaunt
Our bodies
Sharing this mess
Of a world
Together naked in bed

Draping hair on your thighs
The blue of my fathers eyes
Remember the past
We laugh
Recounting the days of our youth
The full moon guides you home
Even after you leave
Can't quite seem to feel alone
Remembering the days of my youth

When it was done to me
So it has been to you
The generation gap closes
Within this kiss
The transmission of bliss
Memories won't we miss
When the days have gone since passed

Laying in bed finally with you
This young woman
Almost all grown up
You will save the world
I see
One country at a time
Indeed
Maybe this full moon
You just start
With me
04/09/09

-Closed Eye Swan Dive-

Heat rises in the bedroom
Like water ready to boil
Air thick with panties
Lip gloss on my pillows
Dead of the night
Desert heat
Stir on top of these sheets
White cotton covered tail
Lips arms frail
Distant thought of jail
Reach the blinds to crack the glass
Let some cool air pass
Something to stir this wave
Of heat & salve this room
Full of love to bloom
Water to plants
No need to wait & see
Everyone's watching
Waiting for you & me
To say something
To each other
To the world
Make some sort of statement
With this bed we have made
So many times your head
In my arms I lay
On top of you the hunter
Writhing deeper together
Like bumper
Cars
We bump thighs, legs
Jogging we sweat
Thighs & edges
Of cliffs, we climb
Paying mantra's

Through time
Together, playing
Like the children we once were
Watching traffic speed by
A kiss of summer
In the corners of my eyes
Suppose I could just let go
This rope burn start to slowly
Heal
As the string takes to the sky
Watch our little red balloon fly
& let go of something called comfort
Letting myself go
Falling over the cliff
Knowing
Willing to fall
With nothing there to catch me
& not a care in the sky
04/21/09

-Look To The Sky-

The sacred geometry of chance
The single unit of dance
Prancing away
Laughing day
Halfway true
Wishing this was you
All the ways the phone sleeps so silent
In a dream whisked by
Forever masking cries
Darling
My beautiful love
Gone past
Flashing through our eyes
Today you dashed
Again and again and again
Always running so fast
Never stopping even to ask
How can I be
How can you see
Me still
The days chosen
Filled with your eyes
Watching your memory
Whisk across the sky
05/05/09

-Sitting at El Matador-

Oh the sun
Sings so loud
Wind playfully
Slapping face
Mind
Smooth as ocean shores
She breaks upon
Perfect rocks
Scatter broken glass
Memories of a thousand storms before
Footprints along the shore
A new vision of love
Opens a door
Breathing in
To where it is beautiful & warm

Sea kelp shadowed surface
Buoyancy life
Tiny islands float
Above the water world below
Pelicans changing lanes
Soaring free like winged planes

Squinting horizon
Salted air neck
How can this be anything else
But God
Everything I see in nature
Harmony

The pain of the past
Waterlogged bogged
Merely floating away
No longer the raft
Once ridden upon

Now just a gentle landing
For fatigued seagulls
& soothing kelp

Its easy to ask for help
When inside is where you go
The ocean
She holds us so tight
Its no wonder
You're always in our sight

Splashing
Washing away
Letting life kiss us this way
Watching these waves break
05/11/09

-The Changing Seasons of my Life-

Old spindles paint the sky
All projections from the times before
Colored floors
Glances from strangers eyes
Little Mexican girls jumping around
The girl with long coal hair
Down the isle leans back
To pour water down her throat
Business men finger fucking blackberries
Tourist scurry
At the sight of the next big scene
Hollywood can be such a dream

Down here under the city heat glare
Tunnels that stretch so far
From decades before
Plotted and planned
The city of angels landed
Long before I ever thought
Of any of this

My train arrives like an airplane
Screaming down the tube
Squeeling brakes
Just the moment it takes
To step inside
These sliding glass doors

Linoleum chocolate
Cupcake floors
Strangers scattered like litter
There's a man
Passed out
Head bouncing gently on the glass
Priority seating for seniors

And disabled
Immediately I'm stabled
Into upside down barstools
Hanging from the ceilings
The loud-speaker mumbles
In seconds I'm humbled
At the sight of our public transportation

Takes me back to Europe in a flash
Dancing through Paris with cash
Was just like a dream
I remember 19
Holding hands next to the seine
With you

The tunnels curve past western
I'm back in the mountains again of Lucerne
Watching the enormous rocky skyline
Pushing me into a long summer
What a bummer
I haven't been across the pond
In almost a decade

I used to promise I'd make it
No matter what the trouble or glory
Nothing else to worry
About
With a back pack and my poems
Ladies, wine and the open road
A whole new world to discover again
On my own

Back in my zone
People are leaving
While my hips just shift with the brakes
Making great time I see
The journey has been so good to me

This morning just thinking
It's not about the destination
But the things I see along the way
The friendships people make
The colors and textures
Of distant days
Taking it all in
This lifetime I wander
An artist
Recording everything I cross

Your face
The sun settling into place
Another dimension
Of time and space
So much stimulation
Such a vibration
Shifting to higher plane
Even on this subway train
05/12/09

-Someone We'll Never Meet-

Warm breeze
Blue sky and palm trees
California my home
So accustomed
Watching helicopters saunter by
They hover and flutter
Littering the sky with a vibrating hum

Taxis hail
Semi trucks wail
I'm quite sure that light was red
Perfect turbine on his head
Baby strollers to the brim
Head turning I win
As she was definitely worth a second glance

The American flag in the distance
Waiving my father
Persistence I keep
As another homeless woman
Shifts by
Toenails as long as emery boards

Ankles dipped in mud
Hair rag jet lagged
She mumbles something
Walking by to a meeting
With someone we'll never meet
Looking down at my own feet
With socks and shoes
Real people to meet
Plenty of rich clean food to eat
So grateful for everything
This time around
05/12/09

-Been The Killer-

Fools in love
Are there any other creatures
More pathetic
So here the story continues
Everywhere
I go now
Everywhere
I come from
This feeling
I bring to the table
The knife
& the heart
The skin
& the blood
The sacrifice
The hurt
The love I feel
I destroy
Every time
This way
I should know
This way
I should know this so
For I have been the killer
My whole life
Whole life hole
I should know
Because this fools
In love again
05/16/09

-She Was Dying Her Hair-

Woke up this morning
Just like every other morning
Felt the difference on my skin
Time to grow again
Expand
Time to land
On a new level
Of consciousness

She brought her to me this time
In my dreams I asked
In my days she came
The wizard of my darkness
The light to the dark
She shed the light upon me
& I found nothing but
Beauty

Woke up this morning
Just like every other morning
Felt the difference in my shame
Time to grow again
Expand
Time to heal
On a new bevel
Of acceptance

Sitting on the couch
Gently slouched and fitting
Depositing stories
Withdrawing reflections
Seeing just far enough behind me
To see the future
The growth is vast
Forgiving the past

Of all the teachers
That came before you

Letting this truly be
The story of me
My sexual desires set free
Transforming society
Plans forming I can be
So hard on myself sometimes

Woke up this morning
Just like every other morning
Felt the abundance in my mind
Time to sow again
Expand
Time to feel
A new level of
Consciousness
05/21/09

-Sitting Duck-

Laying in bed I'm dead
Weight
Against your skin
Fingers running over thighs
I keep them circling
So you won't notice my mind stand
Still
Losing myself again
Losing another friend
Sometimes I make it happen this
Way
Smiling at you so silly
Behind this mask I'm already gone
Just performing these songs
Like the years before
Learned to eat what never liked
Learned to sing what I never heard
Time to run
Off forever
Smiling
see you never

You knocked at my door
Just as I was saying good bye
Giving my final glancing
black stretch pants prancing
walking up to my door
to save me
to kill me
Naked in bed
Panting I'm dead
Ready to walk away from this blonde
This bomb severs
Our bond
It's just too late

in the night
It's just too late
in the relationship
Last week this was nothing
The bird in my hand squeamish
So shrilling
So brilliant
Killing us all at once
So let me get this straight
I'm through with her
You're through with me
Now I'm through with you
Lets just all be through with
Each other-oh brother
Take 248 the search
Back on again
Time to heal
Time to feel
This one might hurt more
Than I have anticipated
The pain in your eyes
Was deep dark
And cold
The shoulder
I must have looked like a stranger
In my own door stoop
Such a creep
Shall we both weep
Or just roll over
Into another coma
No pulse
No heart rate
Just cold body
Weight
Against your skin
Laying in bed dead
05/22/09

-Blackened-

The cold
Covers your eyes painted
Black eye shadow
Blood in the gallows
Flail into the night
Like rain
Dragging on this pain
Banging on my door
Searching for more
Take this flashlight
Search the floors
Under the faucet
Behind these drawers
Find the pain you need
So much

Take this blade so rough
Drag our faces in the dirt
Like chain link fences
Shaking
Making it so much
Easier
To run into the night
Crying
With no need to look back
Shaking so scared
Running
Into a black hole
05/22/09

-No One Sees Me This Way-

Digging mud
Covered in blood
& dirt
Clothes wrinkled, death
Wreaking breath
Lubed slippery fingertips
Passed out still warm
The body in bed
Lay victim

The shovel
In hand
Covered dirt
Moonlit skirt
Double panties
Fantasy galore
This suicide core

Apple in hand, eating
You found me this way
Taking a break from all this
Digging again
The garden
She grows

As you stand outside
My house
Waiting
Watching time unravel
The garden which I show no one
Now exposed
Chemical burns, lye
Dark eyes November
Corpse on limber
You open in shock

Like an aperture
Caught me off guard
No time to wash
Up or clean
Just enough to cover these
Blood stains
Dirt, neck & back
Calloused hands bleed
The face he wears

The garden grows
So much faster than I can keep up with
Knife in hand
Looking around
At all these ditches
So many piles of neatly packed dirt
Hurting again
In the dark
Of the night
05/22/09

Can't you see myself hurting this way

-Haven't I Been Good To You-

Lets make a gravestone for your head
Take the pain of us
Together to bed
Forget me
& the things we learned
Laugh out loud
Another day
Wasted away
Without you here
Causing pain to others
Must be something
I have learned
When did this become
So acceptable
So sustainable
The freeway pass
Shivers in the cold
Santa Ana winds blow
Through lies I have spread
Take me out to the pier
& push me in
Leave me for dead
05/22/09

-Hurt The Ones You Love-

Just look at the mess I've made
The eye of god so magical
The pattern so ordain
Single for summer
I didn't even realize it was happening
Planting the seeds to rip apart
Making phone calls
Breaking your heart
So easy with this knife
All there is to do is cut myself
And watch you bleed
Cut these arms
Cover your clothes bloodied
The voodoo doll
Of suicide
We both lay slain
To my pain
Now you feel me
Now you don't
Now you see me
Now you won't
The nursery rhyme
Perfected in just thirty two
Years
Now go shed tears
05/29/09

-In The Orchard Mumbling-

Maybe I should just tattoo knives
To my forearms
Road signs that lead
To the danger
Off ramps in the hallway
Giving everyone
Every possible
Chance
To escape

The wrath of my black love
The cut so deep
Only hurting
The ones I love
Jagged

I have killed them all
On some emotional level
Stood tall &
Shoved you all
Over
The edge
Took your tears
Thrown to the ground
Made you swear
Never again
& then you do it

Again
You let me in
Deep inside your womb
Your most precious place
I crawl
& betray

The wrath
Of flying, black doves
Only hurting the ones I love
You have one last chance
To leave the path

To escape
The bleeding knives
Before you breathe
The feature
The need
One last chance to leave
Blood covered, latex gloves
Beware, a splintered staff
The wrath of my black love
05/31/09

Sometimes fantasy becomes real life

-806 and The Floor Dying-

806 as she lay dying
Halfway crying
Sobbing
Panting in fear
Nothing in her voice clear
The room filled with heels
Glossy veneers
Swept neatly under
Spring full lips
Lotion parted hips
The message clear
Help me now

I responded somehow
Valet ballet
Elevator dance
Counting room numbers
I glance
804
805
806 the door ajar
Found jarred
In a robe
Laying hair sprawled
Leopard dress on the floor
Arms swaying
& just the raspy noise
Of lungs
Trying to fill with air
What to do
Inspecting the room
A woman lay dying
As I enter and loom
Pill bottles neatly stacked
In the bathroom

Flipped open lids
Water falls from my mouth
Into yours
Swallowing
Wallowing
Asthmatic asthma inhaler
How I longed to see you later
Not even stopping to think
What would it look like
If you just died here
In my arms
A total stranger
Nothing stranger
Than me
Here
Alone in this room
With you
As you lay dying

On the floor
Rationalizing cpr
Broken purse hangs from the table
This expensive room like
A movie scene
In motion and incomplete
four years later we meet
I don't know why I came
Enthralled with life
You don't know why
You called
In your moment of strife
Head cradled
In my arms
Whispering you are safe
Finally
I notice the soft curves
The bridge of your nose

The jaw line so smooth
Even as you lay here
Exhausted
Full of panic
Mumbling so maniacally
Scared but focused
Into your eyes I can see
My how beautiful you truly are
06/04/09

-806 and The Floor Dying II -

Listening to your direction
I continue the inspection
Of the situation
Drawing the line in my head
When to call 911
If you seem to fall
Into any worse state
Risking state prison
A violation indeed
A woman dead on the strip
I see this situation
As dangerous as
Your collapsing lungs
Thrusting hands
Together we lunge
Breathing in
And breathing out
Filling your lips with air
Billowing hands
Your dyed hair pink
On the ends
A little girl's life
Depends
On the decisions
I make tonight
Bringing you back to life
God works in this way
Kissing me now you lay
On the bed
Wanting to reward me so
Telling you that I don't want
To be repaid this way
You disrobe me anyway
Swallowing the city
Outside the eighth floor view

The pool below chatters
Like birds flocking to water
Into the night we go
Twisting our bodies
Make this dough
Kneading and threading
Slow, how l need it to be
These days
Starring like a scarred child
Only seventeen sometimes
I seem
To be, emotionally
Turning us over the sky
Belongs to the night
High above the sunset strip
Into this king suite we dip
Fleshing out what were to happen
The moment we first spoke
On the phone
Fours years ago
06/04/09

-Like For My Father-

Yeah it has been a while
Sitting here thinking
The first night
I stared into your eyes
I knew it then
Something would pierce me
Love at first sight
I'm not sure
So many years later
Life's okay to me
I'm okay alone
Just hard to imagine
The way things turned out
They way we still love each other
Special I guess to share this bond
Is this what is was like for my father
When my mother would flirt with him
At Christmas dinner
Then say goodbye and shut the door
After dessert
Is this what it will be like
When I'm an old man
Guess I should just stay on the positive
Side of things
And just be grateful there is
Even you to think about
What a great time we sure had
06/07/21

-Ms. James-

For I am the hunter
And you are the hunted
Elephant ass
The size of a Texas mass
I glance and pause in bliss
Those giant clouds kiss
In my dreams I fiend
For the cream in your panties
On my lips
So soft the mince of your voice
Carried from the next room
As you whisper baby

Just maybe this time
Perfect kills
Romantic thrills
Of trying again
Inside of you I day dream
Parting your skin
Swimming inside you
Writing on the walls o' your uterus
Leaving nursery rhymes and letters
For unborn children to find
In the future
As they grow in this oven

A bakers dozen
Of years behind me
Living the dream
Besides you running today
I felt a beam
Of possibility in our new found
Friendship
This ship of friends departing
At the dock waiting for this flock

Of honing pigeons to return
This black satin love
A letter written in lemonade
So sweet and pink
Another day of your little piggy
Feet, walking around
The ground floor
Of my lonesome world
For I am the hunter
And you are the hunted
06/10/09

-A Moment In Time-

The museum of death just
Down the street
Looks so interesting from
The outside
Who would want to see
Those things
I guess right now, me

It's a narrow path
The road leads to
So we send our little
Messages to each other
Like kids in class
Folded lined boomerang
If you send one back
Were just friends these days
So with each others feelings we play

The Santa Ana winds blow
Against my face so warm
Like the way you used
To laugh at me loud
& strong, this stoplight
Too short to finish
My thought, traffic
Pushing me on
03/11/09

-How Sorry I Am-

There was just so much I couldn't tell you
I just couldn't let fall
From my mouth
The truth about the things
That you found
The things that I am learning
To accept
I know you know
I could see it in your eyes

I can feel you slipping
Past your dignity
Losing yourself in the sunlight
Of the day
You just keep turning away

Trust the way life pushing us all
Down the river we swim
Splashing and rocking
Crashing onto these walls
We do
Accepting our scars as proof
That we are truly alive
And learning
Scarring we go
Bleeding
And so
06/17/09

-X-

Your brown skin whispers
To me through the sheets
We spin in cycles
Of legs and thighs
Turning over the pages
Of the week
Each day waking next to you
The magic of our lips kissing
My hands on your hips slipping
Downwards, southern drawl
Every night for your longing
I crawl
Waiting for you
In the deep of the night

The earth can stand so still
When I open my eyes to yours
The child inside laughs
Like the children playing
Outside your bedroom
Maybe we'll have to wait
Till you get home
But until then
Without you
I'm alone
Yearning to roll over
To your side of the bed
Kissing the back of your head
Resting in the night next to you
06/28/09

-Bursting In Air-

Dated bills scatter perfect
The fan blowing circles collecting dust
Dishes doing the rounds
Cabinet table sink cabinet
Scuff marking the floors
Repeating this life I do
Growing older like the tree
Watching the leaves of my skin
Change

Calendars blow away
As my eyebrows grey
Only wearing three different
Outfits in a closet filled brim
Don't even tie my shoes
Like lovers
I just slip in
And slip out
Dated relationships
Expiring food
I eat them all
Unconsciously I fall
Into everyone else
Like some dramatic scene
Climaxing in the middle of the
Dance floor
Acting like this is the biggest
Deal in the whole world
The Berlin wall falls
Every night in my mind
Loading the kids
Up for the weekend
Camping out in the living room
Never really getting too far
Away from my comfort zone

Realizing that everything
That I ever wanted
Is just outside the door
Just inside more
Deeper
I must go
Swimming into myself
In meditation
Social observation
Only gets one so far

So unlock the car
And scoot the fuck over
I'm getting in
All of us within
How many voices in my head
Telling me where to go
Can't we just all agree
Pack up and flee
Drive further away and
Burst through
This comfort zone
It's time to expand
About to explode
06/28/09

-Koi Fish Swimming-

& so the bombs bursting in air
The red flag thirsting with flair
The dessert heat
Smothering every pore on our bodies
Infomercials litter the room with fuzz
Big hair, high socks
Doors, clock, lips lock
This fourth of July like a dream
To think this is really how
Free we are just to be
Brown skin together melting
A bowl of flowers and jewelry
On the floor
Angels standing above
Koi fish swimming the air
Jet black hair
Taking our time
In recovery
Under the covers
We recover
Just to discover
One another
Smiling in the hands of time
One hundred miles away
Hidden and stable
Ready and able
To see another day
Watching the sun come up
Through the curtains
Bleed the night away kissing
Missing sleep
Hissing the sound
Of the air conditioned unit
Clicking on and off
Taking off your socks

Crumbling to sleep like
Falling down the hillside
Into the desert we hide
Lovers
For the first time
Finally free
On this fourth day
Of July
07/05/09

-Outside Your House-

& so you leaned into the car
Through the window
To kiss me
Just barely missing me
Watching the clouds saunter by
The silhouette of July
In your eyes
The smell of fear
Creeping from your thighs
I feel the pull
Wanting to get away
But just lean in further
I do instead
Lead in my pants
Hands wet with sweat
The moon catches my eyes
And in an instant
We forgot all our lies
And just smiled at each other
Enjoying a peaceful beat
The summertime heat
Just perfect tonight
Something about your lips
That just makes everything all right
Something about this night
Finally feels right
And so you leaned into the car
Through the window
To kiss me
07/08/09

-On The Edge of A Continent-

At the beach
On your back
I awake
Transported in time
Distorted
Sublime
Like we never said
Goodbye
Years galore
The tears before
The freckles darken
As the sun brightens
Enlightening another day
Wiping your hair away
Wishing there was
Just a single grain of sand
On the beach
That could resemble
The hope I need
For you to ever trust
Me again
To ever open that bridge again
Chewing red apples
Sitting staring
Baffled
Watching the currents
Wondering, how the hell
We ever ended up here again
Feeling the earthquake
Across the globe
Shaking the tides
So high today
I can't remember anything
When I look into your eyes

The profile of love
Thoughts of divinity
Nothing makes sense
The times you kiss me
Over and over again
I fall into you
Year after year
The season so clear
Summers here
And so are you
The beach is softer
But my index finger
Criss-crossing
Drawing circles across
Your back is something
Much more serene
Than anything
I could have ever seen
In the life
We both shoveled
Both redefined
In the life we both left behind
Watching your face change
As the sun starts to wane
Forever could I stay in this day
07/15/09

-Flight Forty Five-

Flying high in the sky
Free and as far as a bird can see
An ocean of blue below
Marshmallow clouds
A frozen tundra below
Leaning out the window
Peeking down
First class
In body and spirit
Everyday I start over
Just to begin again
So many revelations
Inside just ten minutes
A lifetime of thoughts
In just the first cup
Biology
Theology
Ideology
Perfect cup of coffee
Draped in white
Sugar and milk swirl
Oh god I love this world
What an experience
This human trip
With you all
Everything in my mind
I see in the world around me
Truly have I finally
Awakened
To Life
07/25/09

-The Corner Of My Eyes-

I have this vision of you
That's trying to creep through
Across the room
The dark of your hair
Cast this shadow of love
Something coming from above
Against the back wall I see the future
A glimpse of something in the days
Yet to come

Like telling stories
Of when we were younger
Somehow I can see
That we are living those
Stories now
And then
It comes over me

I have this re occurring vision of you and me
Seeping through the willow trees
At dawn
Something about your yawn
That I recognize from the future
Is that you I seem to whisper
To myself starring
From across the room
Your arms just move towards
Me every time we meet
Like clockwork we greet
Each other with smiles for
Tomorrow
But today
I saw it again
Something about you
I have just a clue

But if blink just fast enough
I can still see it through
This re occurring vision
I keep having of you
There is something there
I just can't tell
I'll guess I'll just have to wait
For time
She always tells
08/04/09

-The Oncoming Exit-

So many things racing through my head
You make me feel so much
That I don't want to feel
The youth so painful
All of sudden why am I
Questioning my relationships
With my mother
God it kills me that you didn't
Call today at all
Didn't you see me driving by your house
Missing your soft squishy face
Thoughts of you all over
My work place
Even there you have infected
They all know your name
Your jewelry in the bathroom
Just laughs at me
While pictures on my desktop
Someone just keep opening
I hope things come together
There's something special
About you & I
Moving so strong so smooth
This summer won't tell us lies
Hurry up and finish this week
Before I make up my mind
And let us fall
Off the deepest darkest cliff
I can find
Somehow just before bed
I seem to forgive you
Rest my head knowing
That nothing changes over night
Not even my anger
& not even your sighs

I don't even know what
I am saying
I just know I have to
Express myself
To see where I am
These days
Oh fuck
Women
08/12/09

-Loading Clips-

So many ways show the life
Whispering secrets into this black box
Now the world can take a peek
Out here in front of you all
Not too many seem to care
Even when they can see behind the glass
The mask still sits on the head
The lips still move the words
Growth is internal
& this is just experimental
The way I feel about you
Is something deeper
Than the stoplight
Spacing out the window
Watching the world pass us by
Thinking so clearly
Been years since I been high
Feeling so much more than
I ever asked to feel
This onion keeps peeling
The days stay reeling
I just can't hide these feelings
Any longer
The next level I am willing
To take us there
Out of here
If you want to come
08/16/09

-Kialani-

So we made it past the fall
The cliffs not big enough to break
Us taller than the trees
The clouds seem to be
Just smoke on the glass
I guess I just need to wash
My car more often

Driving away again
You're in the rearview
And the night was perfect
Perfect Thai food
Red-hearted mood
Giddy legs folded
Laughing in the car
Boy I guess we sure
Have come far

Friends for sure
We build this house
That sits upon fertile land
Just two fingers
or my whole hand
Just hold me again
Through the night
As you did the last
Kidnapping me
Making sure that I
Slept well
So caring you are
Listening to you for real
Let's just pretend that
Were not scared
We can stand alone at the top
Spill our guts

And when were still facing
Each other with these truths
Wide open like the road
Maybe there is nothing we need to hide
Maybe there is something about the low tide
That makes the moon pull
So much greater
When those waves come crashing back in

Watching the shores rise again
As the new day begins
I see this relation ship
Growing
On the sunny side
Of the garden
Sitting outside the house today
Not quite a smile
But maybe a fragile smirk
Listening
Watching
The summer flowers
Bloom
08/18/09

-Brothers In Arms-

I think it's finally hitting me
The new life that I have made
I can't believe thumbing through
These pages, the pictures
Of you, the people that
Were so instrumental, in my growth
Your hair is getting so long
Off to Bristol you have gone
Someday soon I shall take a visit
Over the pond and take a gander
A museum, a bakery or too
Some tea time with you

These faces that scatter the earth
My new friends on the berth
The boat rocks so peaceful
This way of life finally found me
What a joyous program
What a loyal showman
God I love living the way
I was always meant to be
Always meaning to be me

See you guys everyday
Our struggles make the way
Teaching me so many times
So much, everything I listen
You walk me home every night
Keeping me safe I sleep with you

I wouldn't trade anything for this journey
Now such a memory
So many times do I hit my knees
Asking for the help
The guidance

Thankful for another day to play
To create, to love
To live, to fully express
God's joy and light
Through everything that I touch
Truly have I been touched

Easy to take the next step
Watching the way my mind talks to me
Sometimes I have to ignore it
When others are so close
I have to be careful where I swing
This sword so strong
Still in my hands
Swinging back and forth
Still swinging back and forth
Falling to the sides
Carefully watching
The night come again
And I have made it through another
Day, somehow I found a way
Not to hurt anyone
Or myself
And just to think
If there was one more chance
To try it all again
08/20/09

Why am I so attracted to that which I just can't seem to reach

Was it something I learned as a child

-But Like My Mother-

Hurting so bad
Touching your skin
Such sin
When your lips
Touch mine

Chemicals release inside my brain
Spectrums of electricity must
Jump from neuron to neuron
Collapsing memory pods
From years before

The storm you bring to mind
The clouds billowing in time
God your eyes burn through
The core of my existence
Every time I see the little kid
Inside of you

Driving your million dollar machine
Touching you so insane
The most giant softest lips
Of all time
You'll never be mine
Why can't I just turn and walk away
Knowing the barbwire is just too much
To take when the spikes crush my hands
Bleeding palms

Fleeing pawns
The characters of my life
Will surely run and cry when I damage them
Surely it will just hurt too bad
To walk away so many times
From you

I must come to you again
To see in the light
Just give me one more memory tonight
Risking the lessons I know to be true
Insanity with you
God you drive me so crazy
But it's still so wrong
Why can't I just sing this song
And let it slide like
The rocks that want to crumble
Standing under this humble
Still mumbling when I walk away
Watching your face in the distance
I see the woman I wish I could hold
But like my mother
I just never could reach you
I never got enough
And sand paper is too rough
To rub across your legs
Bleeding from the head
Mentally aching

I miss the sound of your voice
Calling my name in the sheets
Perfect sleep
A perfect heap of flesh
We make when we lay this way
Something about our brown skin
That just makes sense
Yet there's nothing easy
About you and me

Forging through
Our own eternities
Still alone
Searching for love
And searching for one

Something with someone
Something worth meaning
God you're so good
At leaving me
Quick snap and your gone
Never believing you
Yet this time I must let go
For I know too much
This time around
To pretend otherwise

A fool in love
A cool black glove
To cover my hands
When I lift weights
Some cool black skin
To cover my face
When I have to lift you away
Somehow
Life will take us away
For my love
My Christina
There will be a time
When I must allow myself
To fly away
08/20/09

-This Side Of The Lake-

Midnight black sighs
Scream up to the sky
Caramel tight thighs
I'm not scared anymore
The girl with slanted eyes
Lets move into the next stage
The loft, the gate, the date
Night on Mondays
Kissing through Tuesdays
In the back of the room
Huddled like bread in a bag
In the dark

Lets just have fun today
Take my hand and let go
Of the stress of your day
Just for today we can be in love
For the whole day
We can just hug
And roll around in bed
Let the world slip us by
In the streets
The cars
They just keep coming
Writhe up and down
These feelings
Like oil on water
There's just nothing to bother
When we melt together
When we ride the sheets
The way you stick out your tongue
So hot, the dark, the sweat
We meet like this
Infrequently, just as
We swing back into focus

Loving the way
Your jet-black hair
Falls all over my place
Slide your fragile hand down my face
Kiss these lips
Now aimed true
My ching-chang for you
Loving the moment
When I pull up in front
Of the house
And see you coming out

So beautiful to the eyes
So hard not to cover your thighs
With my leg
When we sleep
Even though you don't like
To cuddle much
We can just double-dutch
This next song and be free
Free to be happy
Free to be you and free to be me
Accepting of you do me

My new best friend
Come
To this side of the lake
Look off into the horizon
There is something
I want you to see
Let us not be afraid
Of the unknown
It's the only place left to go
It is truly the only place
Left for us to go
08/24/09

-The Scent of Rich Soil-

Failed the test
Last night felt the best
Flirting with disaster
Accepting the mission
Numbers passed
And then it happened
Straight into your eyes
I saw the keys fall to the floor
The flood-gates open
And the water
She rushes

Now just the next day
The surreal becomes the real
Just like store bought fantasies
Flesh becomes thoughts
This small bedroom
We draped in sweat
Banging the side of the bed
Into your fake window
The legs crinkle like bags
Of chips
I spread your life apart
Like this

After the shower
Hands on the mirror
Your face bouncing against
The hand soap
Beating you so hard I do
Watching my toes slip
On the linoleum
Getting a better grasp
I just grip into place
Escaping the monotony

Of a five day work week
Just like the old days
I weep

Into the night
Back in the garden
Guess I haven't stayed away
For too long
Had to check on the plants
See what has become of my ditches
Target practice again
In the dark
This small alley way
Of single apartments

Keeping you compartmentalized
I realize I am ready for love
I am ready for something
Deeper than this
There's enough ditches in the this garden
I just want to feel something seeping
To find someone leaping
To find someone who wants to go
Deeper, into the night
Ready to let go
08/24/09

-In Liquid Form Creating-

The house creaks with age
Shutters closed
The paint chips away
When the wind
She blows so hard
Against the night
He stays inside
Just on the other side
Of the wall
Waiting
Until it is safe
To come outside again

This old tree once so grand
Now crooked and leaning
Leaves are a memory
And the monstrous roots
Of a giant, so long ago
Lays to rest upon
This dry scorched
Cracking desert lake bed

The knife so dull
Sharpening against leather
Back and forth
So monotonous, so skilled
Making hot sharp edges again
Perfecting the blade
To slice so true
To slice into you
The blade heals so well
If you just press it the right way
Letting the blood seep so fine
Mechanically divine
The power of humans

In liquid form
Creating the healing
Stealing the life away
So much to do in a day

Peeking out the house
Tip toeing through the blinds
Blinded by mid days heat
Biting down
The wood on my teeth wreak
Of your clothes
Something from the days passed

Knowing I have to leave the house again
To walk those roads outside
Watching, waiting, preparing
For anything that this crazy world
Just might throw my way
Pacing the line
Waiting for the right time
To jump back out
And get back on the road
Alone again

Never escaping my own head
Every day is a lonely bed
Been waiting for years
Maybe this time there is no going back
Maybe this time I won't come back
To this old house
Rugged and torn
Beat down and worn
The shelter from this desert heat
Maybe this could be my last
Retreat

Maybe I should just keep moving
Maybe somewhere down the road
Alone out there in the world
Something
Someone
Is waiting for me
08/27/09

-A Box By The Door-

Packed all your stuff in a box tonight
Your shoes, sandals
Earrings, notes
Pants and jacket
Packed it by the door
With my ego
Just to let you know
I can say goodbye too
In a heartbeat
My ego escapes
And tears it all down

Cause I can see through you
And I can be you too
But this tender experience
To taste the new world
Someone to give a chance to
I give this chance to you

Willing to fall again
The cliff so many times
Reaching out for love
Reaching out for more
This horse still gallops
I suppose I should just
Get back on it
Again

Coming back home
I see your box
Bumping my feet
As I walk in the door
What was I thinking
Throwing all your stuff away
Throwing the past few months away

Giving up is just too easy to do
But building something real
That's what I really want to do
Of course you're confused
Of course you're emotional
You're a woman
And I am a man
So here we stand

Patient and willing
I'll guess I'll just have to wait
Till the blood stops running
Till you come running back
Home to my arms

And when another month passes
I'll have to just forget
About bringing out the box
Your shoes are too cute
To give back anyway
How are you supposed to have
Choices when you come over
If I give them all back
08/25/09

-The Way The Shovel Falls-

And so I feed again
The way it comes
Sometimes I don't even ask
Are they tests
Or gifts
She brings them to me
For reasons I can't grasp
The way the shovel
Falls to my hands

Laying here naked
I pant away
Smoking my pipe this old way
Still using after all these years
Trading powder for thighs
The lighter is your eyes
The black satin sheets
An ocean of escape

Laying here
Drifting
Floating away
Even if it is just for a few moments

Doesn't matter what your name is
You have no name
You're just another plot
You're just another pot
Hole in the road
Traveling towards tomorrow
Lost in space
And lost in time
Guess I just had too much on my mind
Today

Another reason to escape
Another tragic date
These bodies just pile
Another reason to hate
The way they all come and go
Feeling myself yearning
Feel the whole world burning
To make some kind of personal change

Some kind of worldwide pain
This bedroom has seen too many
Hands touched by thousands
A heart only touched by few
Guess I'm still just tucking away
These distant memories of you
09/05/09

-Reseal Everything-

This city's killing us
Can't you see it
Smothering laugh lines
Between you and me
Can't you see
The river rising so high
Creaking at the wooden beams
In the dead of the night
The house sleeps
As our dreams, they wander

Last week you were cocked and loaded
This week I don't get a response
The finicky way of Venus
Never understanding your ways
Just the way your hips gyrate
Through the room
I stay mesmerized

Kill the lights tonight
Keep us separated by street signs
And flashing lights
All through the night
Between us
So many miles leaped up
Can't you see
This city's killing us

Haunting my sleep with the voice
Someone I can't seem to see
Thoughts of just living this life
With me
I got your politely written letter
Probably sponsor approved
Dotted I's and perfectly crossed T's

Letting you rest with your exit
From me
Letting your self close the door
From your side of the room

Something I have never been to good at
Learning from you even in the end I do
I guess this relationship is through

Finding a roach on the counter
I scour as I walk in the dark
Spraying and wiping away
Reminding me to leave a note
For the maintenance man
To come and reseal everything

Life's metaphor for boundaries
Resealing all the gaps
Between sex and friends
Between sex with friends
Between ex's and men
Finding myself learning to say no
And feeling okay with it

Lets just move forward
Last night in prayer
On my hands and knees
Back row of the sweat
Drenching at the heat
Feeling the drums beat
The Indian song depletes
Wash the summer
Praying our life complete
Letting go
And letting god
Take us away

As long as I share this with the world
I seem to keep on okay
Letting all beneath these scars
Keeping me clean
Away from those jail bars
I travel the same way I headed
Into the night
Floating
Flying
Aiming with all my might
Traveling through
Feeling the Fall
On the tips
My fingers

They reach for you
Oh winter take this pain away
Just like last year
Wash it all away with your winds
Rinse me down the street
For this city
It's killing us
09/16/09

134

-The Child Inside-

Dead sea scrolls
Once I read
Along the swift currents
Of the red sea
Pounding so hard
The salt in the air

Waiting for you to come home
The fantasy so well grown
Years of thought waves
Hating mopping the kitchen floors
So many boxes to put away
Closets full of clothes
Never worn anymore

With my eyes closed
I call your name
As my eyes
They get weaker
So much quicker reaching
For my glasses
The jewelry just seems to grow

On my arms with the ink
Tattoos of memories
And milestones
Sometimes it's so hard
To just not think
Sometimes it's so hard
To quiet the mind

Keeping focused and excited
A daily goal I reach
The checkered flag
Waves inches in front of my face

Every day a new experience
I meet
Pondering a life away
Waking through tall cities
Buildings
The size of mountains
Wondering
Where my wife is tonight
Crossing the oceans of history
Flashing the scenes
Of fallen civilizations
Romanticizing
A well earned death
Curiosity of that barrel
The final click
And just a mess

The sun rising over the pyramids
Reaching for the stars
Our society of swollen
Hearts and packed filled bars
Cars crashing, babies are born
Let the birds fly south
For the winter
As I go deeper
Inside
For another hundred years
I go deeper
Inside
09/16/09

-Destroy You-

When I disappear
When I
Reach the repair
Into thin air
You will remember
The days when I waited

Over the phone I hear you call
Your human suit still lets you fall
Holding back
The years we would spend together
Why do I need such re assurance
So much insurance on this
Policy
Together
We already carry

So sick of your ways
You never tell me to stay
Why do I want to hear you
So bad

Leaving you so sad
The years that I just couldn't jump
Fucking journey
Confusing as hell
Is this what a lifetime of hell
Would be like

So in that crowded place
I found you again
Texting messaging and then
We chatted for a few minutes
I was lifted away
Surrounded by flashing lights

And spilling drinks
Just feeling your words
Still makes me think
There could be something
Beautiful between
You and I
So like pink and purple eyes
You stay squinting at the sky
And just keep playing the way
You do
And I just keep being me
Only to find each other
Every now and again
This way we do
Darling, yes I want to destroy you
Yes I want to bestow you
Blessed be the best of you
Blessed is the best of me
One day you'll be my
Silver box of music
My ballerina spinning
Gently to sleep
Someday you'll be my
Silver music box
Until then
Darling
I want to destroy you
09/24/09

-Sun Yellow-

We work so hard
Day in and day out
Slaving to the grind
A life finally I lead

Blond hair summer
Flying free strong baby bird
Your motorcycle got ticketed
Tonight
That just doesn't seem right
Longer legs
Smooth skin
Darkened eyes
Beaming June
Just can't seem to keep a straight
Face when I see you seeing me

So under this tree we lay
Asleep with the fall
Autumn keeps us warm
As I roll over and feel you next to me

The morning comes and then you're gone
Not really sure when you'll be back
Thought for sure
It would be a few days
At least

Crawling into bed tonight
I see the sun yellow hair
Resting so peaceful
I guess your back already
Little bird
Your back already
And I know we will sleep well tonight

So play your dreams
And I'll play mine
Rolling over in the middle of the night
Feeling our bodies getting used to each
Others, pretty soon we will need this

Pretty soon little bird
We will need this
10/10/09

One day at a time

Slowly as if for the first time

I turn myself within

And begin again

-Fall Children-

Start the winds of change
The little cut on my thumb
Heals itself
No words from you
Soothe the pain now
Just another day
Watching it all change

Feed the animals
For they sleep so silent
Tonight
Under the oak tree's
The stars kiss the moon

Smoke rising in the morning
The new day awakens
To begin the journey
Of brittle wood
And oak turned tables
Upon this altar
I kneel for you

Dripping candles
The scent of fresh sage
My fingernails grow
From day to day
Inside my mind
No longer gray

Every time I pray
I seem to grow
Every time I pray
I seem to heal

Remove the bandages
From our eyes
For the skies have cleared
Tiny drops of dew cling
To the leaves
Of the new season

Here again
The fall children dance
I used to have something
To live my life for

Now I just return to
The start
Returning to the things
That are in my heart

All of this
Just for you
My secret obsession
Of needing so much attention
The story still grows
Page after page
As I grow old
10/11/09

-One Day In October-

And the rain
She came to me again finally
Waited all year to feel this wet
Waited all year just hear your dance
The puddles muddle
As I mumble the words
Of romance

Driving slow
The whole world brake lights
Every corner in Los Angeles
Seems to flood in an instant

These memories of life
Inside my head
In an instant
So filled

Falling asleep to the rain
Something of love
Something so soothing
The calming way
The sky cries

The tears of the gods
Plummet to my face
The tears of the world
Cleansing this place
Oh winter this way she comes
10/13/09

-When The Night Comes-

Sitting at the bar showing off
My non alcoholic beer taste the same
As the old days do
But your face is nothing old
Just new and refreshing
My new night-time friend

Past the big hands
By the time
We get together
To play and poke
I lean over just to rest my face
In your neck
It's the tiny hairs that
I'm aim for
But I guess a kiss
Just slips out as well
Puckered lips
Coconut bliss
My little fuzzy penguin
I want to swim in your oceans

Eating tofu and curry
Seems like now there is no hurry
Our friendship has grown
To something comfortable
My hand on your leg
Your fingers in my side
The waitress wonders
What part of the story
Were on
I guess I am too
I know it's something near
The beginning
But what the role, I just can't tell

But when night falls tomorrow
I know you'll be close by
My midnight lover
Stay by my sides
For the winds of change are here to stay
And a dark long winter
Is surely on it's way

Keep me warm till November
And I'll stay faithful
Through December
Just know that when January arrives
A new version of you and I
Will be patiently awaiting

Midnight lover
Stay with me tonight
Cause there's something
So right
About leaning over me
In the morning,
Stretching, reaching
For the alarm clock
By the time
The new day rises

And when I first open my eyes
Midnight has turned to morning
And through another level
We have come
Midnight lover
Stay with me this morning
Let us watch the world, start their day
Oh Midnight lover
Let's just sleep in all day
10/16/09

-Man Of Valor-

So much stimulation
My world rang so loud
Pounding and distracting
The day aches to just awake

Sunlight to bright
No coffee in sight
God I needed you today
And you were there to listen

The gift recovery has given to me
Never any dust collecting
For I use this tool too
Often to let stand still
The gift of an SOS
The ask for help
And you shall receive
I love the way my life
You perceive and collect
Innocent data
Just to read it back to me
Listening intently
How did your words
Become my salve

How did you become my gate way
To healing
Relieving the feelings
That I don't want to feel
Helping me live my life
So real
Together we reveal
The truth of us all
That nothing is impossible
When we work together

So happy that you answered
I just have to express my gratitude
My father my mother
My sister my brother
My friend my sponsor
You are a man of valor

And I am just so dam grateful
So thankful that you have
Come to help

So here I am at the end of another
Tough day
Another rough way
To the bathroom in the morning
And now the night has fallen
And my eyes feel heavy
Today was a good day
I needed help and asked

And so tonight I sleep the sleep
Of the righteous
10/20/09

-Behind My Eyes-

Working so hard like you dad
Wishing you were here
To finally see
Your boy has become a man
I am known across the land

Keeping to myself
I walk home at night
Hiding my cigarettes
So the homeless don't have to ask
Smiling at the lives
Swimming by
Sometimes I think
To myself
Maybe I'm just barely getting by

Feeling the calm and the quiet
Of a stable empty home
Just want my pillow and some water
Count my cash and hide it under the mattress
I guess I am wearing my glasses
More than I want to admit
I guess living alone
Isn't always easy
But most of the time
Rewarding

Halfway down this road
The dusty trails; kick up in heaves
Plans of more travel still up my sleeves
Finally let go of you all
Finally let go of you
Nothing left to fill this void
I feel inside
The emptiness behind my eyes

Because I wouldn't trade it all
For anything
This is the journey I always
Knew I would take
The inner exploration
Of expression

The days turn to nights
And like you dad I slave
Freeways and coffee cups
Gas station receipts
Handshakes and flirts
My days in the city
Are filled with concrete happiness

My loneliness keeps me warm
It surrounds my nighttime
With down comforters and soft pillows
Stuffed animals to talk to
And the corner of my pillow
Takes me home

Still just a kid I see
Still just me being me
10/24/09

-Silence Of Beauty-

Glancing over my shoulder
It's the faucet
Seems to be dripping
Faster than yesterday
That pitter-patter
Against the sauce pan
In-the-sink.

Sounds like the rains
That have yet to come

Sounds like I have yet to acknowledge
The fact that yes
My dear
I have steered us here once again
To this barren place in the pasture
Where the grass is worn
From my knees
Under this oak tree
Where I have rested so many times before.

This place that I have been before
Finding another path to take
The fucking faucet keeps dripping
Pulling my mind away
To the sink
Won't let me think
Just the drip
Of life
Slipping away
Down the drain
Drown the pain
Count the frames
Of pictures
Running around my mind

Of all the woman I have tried
Over the past few years

Back when I was in active
I was cruel, rough and smooth
Getting everything that I wanted
And hurt everything I touched
Since I have been clean
I can't seem to hold a woman
Down for more than a semester

Even a trimester would be nice
Couple months to suffice
I seem to be so willing
And so easy to trust
Fighting the lust on the inside
I seem to keep above these currents
That desire to pull me under

Now once again, ready to move on
Fuck you all and push on
Not gonna let anyone in
I'm too good for you all
Don't you see
You can't be with me
Not even me

I just talk back to myself all day
In the car and the bathroom
Pushing shopping carts
And jogging down the hill
Just the voice in my head
Telling me when to jack off
And fall back to sleep
Just the sound of you and me
That keeps me awake
Through the night

Now there is no one
No person to put in this hot seat
In the center of the room
No electric chair to stare
Just the silence of beauty
And myself
Creating this life

So long have I lived alone
The child of responsibility
I built my own home
And a small fortune

Maybe just closing myself off for a while
I'll try it for a couple of weeks
Guess I should leave another
Note for the landlord
The dam faucet
It won't stop dripping.
11/08/09

Just like our love

I make believe

-Newcomers and Prostitutes-

I think I was reaching
For the vegan spring rolls
When I said it
"She's a prostitute man"
Eyes aimed down
Old school-frown
I have to smirk
And grin
Cause if I don't
I just might break into
Tears

Three years of fears
Closing in on me
Close to using I ask
Myself before he can
How much more of this
Can I with stand
Before my disease
Gets the upper hand
And sends me back
To front row land

Start throwing sand
In the air
No sand castles
Just plumes of dirt and dust
Fucking boundaries
Between lust and love
Lost in the middle
Of a thrust and a shove
Working so hard on so many levels
Of my life
Yet it's you in the night

Who I want to be next to
The woman I have known for years
All the tears from the world
Splatter, splash and smear
And run off the umbrella
You cover me near
Never needing to grow
I can just sow
And sulk
And slumber

A whole year of December
In your arms
This winter barn
Miracle charm
Only been since Friday
And already I miss your arms
Your hips at my side
Those little waking eyes
In the morning
Asking me how do I feel

Man, I'll tell you how I feel
Alone and deserted
Spiritually alerted
That I deserve to love myself
The way I have been trained
Knowing and accepting
That the best for me is beyond
This tiny rock of solitude
That I keep choosing
To stay afoot
So let's just say a foot

Or two closer
Is just maybe a little too
Close for you and me

Because when you're in the room
My whole world goes boom
And then it's gone
It's just me and you and your thong
And all I want is between those thighs

South American eyes
When you run your fingers
Through my hair and rub my ears
I might as well be five years
Old and full of preschool tears
The way mommy used to put me down
That's the way I feel when
I come home and you're around
But you see

I came home tonight
You see
And your no where to be found
Probably a few drinks down
A couple pills and a little town
Thousands of miles
Stretched between you and me
And money, and years, and men
Clients and gears
Shifting, paths drifting
Away, further
We stray
I am saddened to say

That when one door closes
Another one opens
Cause here's hoping
That this new season
Gives me the joy and the reason
To jump out of my little black box

This small little chicken pox
Of a room I keep walking into
Not the body or the hair
The right words
The perfect stare
I want the woman who won't let go
The woman who can't say no

To integrity, self respect
Never expecting a check
For something that she didn't feel
Completely right about
So let me do my own about face
So let me do my own without a trace

Just skip up and out of place
Learned enough
But now clear
The only game I'm playing
Is Truth or Dare
With loving eyes you show me
And I no longer need to use
Even when I want to
Cause I already learned

A new way to live
There's never a reason
To back peddle and skiv
Along the shores of the past
Cause like the tattoos
On my forearms
Today I bear the arms
Of a man who's walked through flames

I walked through fire
And I walked through

Pain, and even though
I miss my Street Fame
That shit's changed
And I'll never be the fucking same
And even through this rough patch

Of briar's brush
I refuse to keep these wounds a hush
Cause I know it's the secrets
That'll take me down
So I tell you what
I'm going through
I share this pain with you again
So I can dip this soft green spring roll
And look you in the eyes
And tell you man, yes I have stepped
Aside, that man, I'm using again
And this time is hurts
She's been gone for five days
And I'm going through with drawls
My heroin

My heroine
Man I'm going through with drawls
And I don't like this space
Like the 405 any time of day
This game I just don't want to play
I want to feel the love that I deserve
I want to be the man that I insure
Every time I kneel down on my knees
And pray

Every day when I bless myself this way
Please god I am asking you tonight
Please give me the courage
And the strength to make it through
Another night

Alone
Cause I don't want to use
I don't want to pick up
Whether it's a pipe
Or whether it's you
Cause just like your job
Pays you
Man, I sure pay the price
Every time I spend the night
Laying in bed next to you

It just hurts to be without you
Like sugar to a diabetic
Thirty six days without you is hectic
And then add on to the fact
That you're just the same
As new comers and prostitutes

Small cities, small parachutes
Might as well jump off a barstool
And try and fly
They way I limit myself
With these lies
Why not pick a bigger cliff
Why not pick a brighter sky

Why not pick anything
Besides just getting high
Shape shifting
And face lifting
What in the world am I thinking
I am just barely learning
To love myself
Let alone
Trust in this wealth
That now surrounds me
In every angle of the room

The perfect job
The perfect gloom
Figure and health
Long hair and bedroom eyes
Now if I can just
Get out of my own way
I think I feel some new character
Emerging and trying
To fill this empty room
No need to wait
For the next rainy day in June
I think I'll just stop, center myself
Sit here and bloom
11/10/09

-The Way You Say My Name-

And so it's through this phone
That I hear you, distant
So far you sound
Saying my name like
A total stranger
Like we never made love
Like we never felt anger
When we didn't get our way
With each other

Just like we never woke up
With each other
So many times before
Like I never saw
Your silhouette in the door
Walking back to sleep
From the bathroom
Finding your side of the bed
Finding another reason
To rest my head
Against yours
So many times to you
Have I crawled

You know it takes courage
To call you
In the middle of the night
It takes courage
To hold you
With all my might
In the black
In the light
I guess you just don't see me
The way I see you

The way I see through
The clear plastic glaze
Glazed over your mask
Glazed over your cocktail flask
Dancing through the night
Coming home to nothing
A hollow shell of an existence
Somehow hoping
To believe these words I spill

To get over you sooner
This rollercoaster shrill
Now just a tired moan
I moan at the moon
It's shown
My way home
And it's just sad tonight

Holding this phone
Listening to a voice
I don't recognize
Speaking words
Feeling things, I
Just don't want to feel
You say my name like a stranger
And it's hard to bite the anger
Into my own phone
In my own car
Your face in my head
But your voice so far
And it hurts
To know
That so many miles away
You really are
Just so far
So far away
11/16/09

-Chicken Legs of Taboo-

Wish I could tell you something
Different
Wish I could show you something
Worth sharing
Wish I could feel something
Other than this familiar pain
My old school-gain
To go outside
And watch the house burn down

Taking my time
Spending so many nights alone
Just renting DVD's and junk food
I guess this is what they mean
By growing old and lonely

Some lover cursed me years ago
Told me this would happen
Now like a gypsy curse
I unravel
To the witches brew
The black pot stews
And steams
And chicken legs of taboo
Curse me till dawn
The version of lie I told
The lesson of pain I sold
The days of my life
Withering away in solitude

Often thinking I deserve this
For all those legs I spread
All those heartbreaks I lead
The way to tears
And Sunday morning hugs

Now just killing bugs
On the counter
I pout
And shuffle
And wear my heart
On my sleeve
I can't believe
How easy it is for you to leave

How can I get back on this horse
When I hate this fucking horse
I hate the stable
I hate this hay
Can't I just throw this poem away
And come back to myself
Some other way

Can't we pretend this is real
Can't we pretend this isn't molten
Steal in my hands
Branding myself this way
Waking up to wounds
In the morning
Always telling myself it was you
When the whole time it was
Just me
Hurting myself
Over And over
And over again
Can't I ever pretend
This was anyone else besides
Me
Rationing out these wounds
Over and over
After all these years
11/16/09

-Just Look Black-

The magazines clutter on the dinner table
The kitchen sink
Dripping harmony
Tinkering away
As winter
Comes slithering down
My street at night

Feel like punishing myself tonight
Hurting something
Sacred inside of me
Destroying something
Precious
Just so I don't have to feel
What it's like

Time to cut the veins again
Let the blood seep today
Time to tear myself away
The only way left
For me to run and hide

Time to hit the dirty
Old grimy shack in the back
Time to peel open those rusty
Doors, reaching, leaning in
Waving in the black
Hands making windmills
In the dark
Reaching for a shovel
Heading out to the garden
In the middle of the night

Lets go do what were good at
Let's go make some surface

Level attraction
Some over rated
X rated distraction
Let's go peel some legs
Crack some thighs
Let's go look someone
In the eyes
And just look black

Suck the life from you
Drain you of your age
Let me remind myself
How strong I can be
When I put my energy
In the wrong place
Let me remember what
It's like to try and forget
The way your face tastes

A shovel and some gloves
Work boots and a deep shove
Off to the garden we go
11/16/09

Take me home and leave me there

-Seat Belts In The Night-

I just know there is something
Special about the way we treat
Each other when were left
To ourselves
Just us alone
And your white shelves
Your soft satin gloves
Stay folded, perfectly wrapped
In white cord to the walls
My toothbrush waits so patient
Jumping on your bed
Like a child
We squeeze and hold so tight
Like seat belts in the night
You demand that I roll
Over when you do

I never chose this path with you
I never even chose you
But something inside of me
Has this pull
This rudimentary lull
The way your skin taste
Like water
And you hair is the air
And I let my hands surf
The wind
Out the window
On the freeway
I stay spaced out
And glazed
Sometimes taking days
Just to think about
How much stuff we
Really could do together

If there was someway
To hold this fragile flame
Through these November rains
To be the picture
And the frame
But deep down
I know sometimes
It's cities that pass us
And days when you
Don't even say my name

Sometimes I think
I'm crazy and this is all in my head
You act so surprised
When you hear it
You're like what and how
And I'm like here and now
And together we both pretend
That this isn't real
But deep down
I remember
The way I used to be
The lovers
That I refused to see
The ones
That were, just too real
When I wasn't ready

And so beautifully distracted
Like glass being compacted
We shatter and crumble
Every time you leave town

And so the cycle begins again
We start over as friends
You talk to me even further than
Before, holding these hoops

I must jump through
Then the kisses and then the hugs
The strength of the drugs
Oh they're just too good to say no

Then suddenly
I wake up
Startled
In the middle of the night

And I'm there
And you're here
And were together
And nothing else matters
And the world stops
And my toes wiggle
I just lean in closer
All I can feel
Is your warm
Soft brown skin
You take a breath
And your hand finds mine
Encloses and then time
Just stops
I can't remember anything
And I close my eyes
11/26/09

-From Your Mouth-

And so here we are
My favorite time of year
The trees wilt with snow
The air crisp as glass
You prefer the easy way
It's the harder road I walk
Still looking down over the edge
To see if that is you bending the corner

For everything I do
I know there is some grand plan here

When everything else seems unclear
At least this I know

Cause the world owes me nothing
So we owe each other the world

So walking keep still
Hands in my pockets
Mind of memories fill
Watching the road
Wind its way home
Waiting
For something to fall
From your mouth
12/04/09

176

-Oh Birdy-

We work so hard
Laughing and poking along
Flirting and dancing
The room knows this now
My feelings overflow
When I look into your eyes
I just want to grab
All the things
That you fear
And hold you so near
Your neck, my bridge
Your shoulders
The ridge
Your ears
I park next to
And just sit here
On your shoulder
And wait
For you to
Let go
Of all the things you fear
Just come closer
And near
Cause I just
Want to hold
You
I just want to feel you
Sitting here on your shoulder
I wait
12/05/09

-Inside Your Arms-

Just come home
Please
Just come back for a while
I won't cry too hard when
You have to leave again
I'll try not too

Just give me a few more weeks
Give me some sort of fix
I'll trade you this scar
For a week
Maybe something far
Away can save us
Maybe another night
With the candles
By our side
A bubble bath
And some wine
Something to ease this mind

Soften the world if you will
Just come back by my side
So together we can run
And hide
For winter is here
And this is the time for love
This is the time for us
I'll be right there when you call
I'll be right there in the night
Just come home
I'll be waiting up all night

Maybe just a simple morning
Under the covers
Is all we need to uncover

These simple children
Hiding inside of
You and me

Maybe some other day
Is all we need
Together to knead
As one
To heed and herd
Bleed and blur
The lines where our skin
Intersects and our hands
Touch, something deep
Inside of me
Something so much
A rush of passion
When you open that door

Letting these snowflakes
Flutter, the soft white floor
There's not too much to say
And it doesn't matter
Cause we don't have to say
Anything to feel this love
We don't ever have to speak
Your hair so full
And just your eyes
Allowing me to walk
Inside your arms
I fall so far
12/05/09

www.ingramcontent.com/pod-product-compliance
Lightning Source LLC
Chambersburg PA
CBHW030929090426
42737CB00007B/365